Money Making MACHINE Telecoms

JOY BEST

Copyright © 2017 by MMM Publishers
All rights reserved. This book or any portion thereof may not be reproduced or used in any manner whatsoever without the express written permission of the publisher except for the use of brief quotations in a book review.

Printed in the United States of America

MMM Publishers, 2017

Introduction

This book is based on more than 18 years of experience in the VOIP field in all the different areas including technical implementation, commercial activities and software development. I travelled vastly from the initial study in a UK university and visited many countries of Asia, Middle East and Mainland Europe. The travelling experience showed me different countries are at different stages of the Telecoms development. Telecom markets vary from country to country and if one is able to identify the right market then there is potential for making fast money with little effort.

This book will enable the reader with many benefits which are practical and will open up endless opportunities to make money fast in this most lucrative industry of telecommunications.

The Book goes through a practical based step-by-step guide and at the same time guiding the reader through all the stages of VoIP implementation. My study of business studies coupled with the technical experience of VOIP gives emergence to a unique book which has no comparison in the market.

No doubt this book is money making manual and many of my students today are successful multi-millionaires enjoying the fruits of VOIP. This is an industry which is a fundamental need of society since the need to maintain communication in this digital age is extremely important and a gateway to the new digital social lifestyle.

Many topics are discussed in this book from among them the fast money making techniques, VoIP fraud and how to prevent that, best equipment , best billing software , reputable companies, trade fairs, online forums, online marketing, brand development and financial security.

The reader also access to consultancy via email thus enabling him to practically approach this trade with full confidence and determination.

This book contains a lot of beneficial tips for everyone, whether it is a new investor, a Telecoms company, Sales Managers, Technical experts or those who want to make some serious fast money.

This manual is great help tool for a complete novice; anyone can come into this industry without any prior qualifications or experience.

Contents

Introduction

Potential of VOIP

VOIP trade – commercial activity

VOIP – buying and selling

VOIP - Retail trade

VOIP - DID numbers

VOIP – Mobile Based Apps

VOIP – Software

VOIP - Hardware

VOIP - the Premium Number market

VOIP – Fraud and ways to detect it

VOIP - PBX Hacking

VOIP - Security

VOIP - Financial fraud and how to prevent it

Online Marketing

Online Branding

- Reputable companies
- Trade Fairs
- Practical Step-by-Step for VOIP termination
- Practical Step-by-Step for VOIP Origination Calling Cards, Sim Cards
- New Techniques- Mobile based Origination and Termination
- Cost Analysis
- Rate of Return: Economic Analysis
- Common Mistakes
- Investment Required – equipment, software and purchasing power
- Geographical based trends
- Real Life Examples of Success
- Sample Business Proposals
- Conclusion

Potential of VOIP

VOIP is the abbreviation for the protocol Voice Over Internet Protocol (VoIP).

Today you will find that most of the voice traffic worldwide is transmitted through this mode (VoIP) as it is most cost effective and high quality. Traditional methods of voice travelling through the PSTN network and the Satellite method for International calls are dying out. The PSTN network is very costly to maintain and it has no benefits over the VOIP network. For international calls the traditional method was the voice travelling over Satellite which caused lags in transmission which resulted in jitter, distorted speech due to voice packets clashing and not reaching the destination.

Today you have fast internet connections which are more than capable to support voice based transmission without compromising any quality. VOIP transmissions on the commonly used G723.1 and G729 based voice codecs require no more than 10kpbs of internet bandwidth. This type of bandwidth is available worldwide and the world is now connected on fiber optic and the days of dial-up internet on 33.6 kbps modems are extinct. With ever-improving Internet bandwidth quality the VOIP industry will only grow. With VoIP growth inevitable it means the market is worth billions of dollars.

All the Major Telecom Operators are interconnected with each other on this Internet Based protocol (VoIP) and this literally opens the door for every new setup to interconnect with the largest Telecommunications carriers and thus utilizing the best possible quality. The world's largest International Voice Carrier namely TATA Communications will open account for any entity which buys credit worth of $2000 only.

The monopolization of the world's National Based carriers is breaking up very fast and at the same time the Oligopoly of the Worlds International based carriers. The industry is worth billions of dollars and the proof is that the one of the World's Richest Men established his business in the Telecoms Industry having started from a state of zero. Mexico's billionaire, Carlos Slim made most of his fortune from the Telecoms Industry.

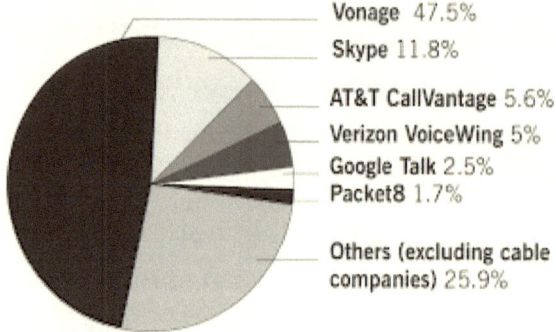

This is the American market for Voice Minutes and it shows the larger companies are dominating this field. It is possible to compete with these companies and undercut them in terms of pricing and still make a healthy profit.

VOIP trade – commercial activity

There are many VoIP services an individual or a small company can market and setup. Each of them is very lucrative and the demand for these services is exponentially increasing. Some of the services that one can look into are as follows:-

i) **Wholesale Minutes**- this involves buying from a Company X minutes at a specific rate. Then add on some profit and resell it to another company the route. So many small carriers will only have limited traffic to destination Y so therefore you sell to each of these carriers route to destination Y and buy this destination from a Major wholesale carrier or direct route provider.

ii) **Retail Origination**- this means to make a platform to sell online minutes direct to the customer through online payment mechanisms. For this only a Branded Dialer and Billing Software is required. Marketing can be done through the local retails shops or online marketing techniques. An interconnection with A_Z Tier 1 carrier needs to be made such as TATA, IBasis, Sprint, Belgacom and then a margin added and retailed to the customer. This is a lot cheaper than Direct Calls from the Mobile Networks or from the Home Based PSTN networks or from the Large Telco's. So therefore there is high potential of making fast money and the rate of return is very good.

iii) **DID numbers** – These are international Numbers which can be mapped onto IP devices or to other Mobile Operator numbers. An example is a USA DID number +17178343323 this can be mapped onto any IP device anywhere in the world or to any mobile number anywhere in the world. This feature allows small companies to have access to world markets and participate in the local business sectors in the various countries. The portal for the DID Numbers market is DIDX.org.

iv) **Premium Numbers** – this is very similar to the DID numbers market however the fundamental difference is that any calls on these numbers will result in a payout at a specified rate. For example if the number is like 449005453343 or 447004554 thereafter every call on these numbers will result on a payout. So if a person calls on this number for duration of 5 Mins only the one receiving the call will get a payout of $2.50 for this call. So this means there is high potential in this market and fast money making scheme if traffic can be generated to these numbers. There is also payout based on per call and not per min so if there are 100 calls on this particular premium number then the payout is $100. So if one can generate this traffic or offer exclusive consultancy services or any other decent technical expertise service then he can get a decent payout.

v) **VPN services** – for many deployment of the VOIP devices worldwide requires VPN connection to overcome the blockage on the SIP 5060 Ports.

vi) **Billing Services**- this is software which will allow the buying and selling of the aforementioned services. A person can buy one license and then sub-license this service thus enables resellers to generate traffic and hence profit.

vii) **Servers Hosting**- A server with a fixed IP address is required to host the Billing Solution and to make interconnections with the Carriers.

VOIP – buying and selling

Buying and Selling VoIP minutes are the easiest method and access to this field. Here we will go through the practical steps in order to achieve the desired results.

Buying and Selling has to be initially done with precaution so that the relationships are built and trust is gained.

The Steps to the taken are as follows:-

1) Get a Hosted server with Billing system which is available for as low as $100 per month. A decent Billing system is which is UNIX based since the Operating System is more stable and not prone to common breakdown or virus attacks or hacking. Avoid those Billing Systems which are Windows Based such as

Voipswitch this is low grade stuff. Better option is Itel Billing system by Reve Systems. The Billing system and the Hosted Server will come with free Technical Support so then the only concern is Commercial related issues.

2) Once the server is allocated you will have a unique IP which you can use to interconnect with other carriers while buying or selling. Buying or selling only requires exchange of IP, defining the rate per minute in the billing system and lastly the credit amount allocated.

3) The next issue is to find a unique route to any country or mobile network which has demand and can be sold in the market. To identify these types of routes you will need to look at the demographics in your country or general migration data. For example you will find there is a lot of demand for African countries, Mexico, Indian Subcontinent, Iraq, Iran, Syria, Philippines and China.

4) Once you have identified a particular route then go onto the online forums and add all the contacts into your Skype ID and similarly find the online VoIP directory and write to the companies asking to buy and sell Route X. Once you have a database of contacts then you need to engage with every person and exchanging lists of routes in demand and routes for sale. Some of the forums are as follows:-
    - Voipforums.com
    - Forumvoip.com
    - Calltermination.com
    - voip.forumfree.it/
    - ukvoipforums.com
    - globalvoipforum.com/

5) Armed with a database of contacts you need to make persistent contact with the different carriers, persevere with this and not lose hope. The fruits of patience are always sweet.

Once you have identified a carrier who is selling you a route less than the market rate for it then firstly test the route from your Mobile or IP Dialer. There are many IP dialers available in the market for free.

6) After the successful testing of the routes agree the payment terms with the seller if it is small unknown company offer to pay him (post pay)daily through PayPal or other online payment methods. Likewise ask the route buyer for a small deposit or give him some small amount of credit after having verified his credentials and even a Google search of his IP, his email address and name will show the type of client he is. If it is larger company with an established business profile then you can be relaxed and agree the terms for payment whether it is weekly or bi-weekly.

7) Now let the traffic starts the clients will send you traffic to your IP and you will then direct to your terminator providers IP. After this the next step is basically to monitor the daily traffic and wait to issue the first billing invoice. On this first invoice you will know how much profit you have made.

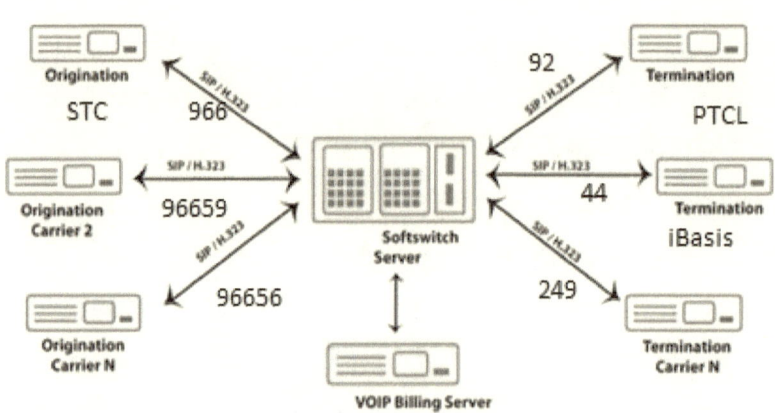

This chart shows the importance of the VoIP technology and how it is replacing the TDM form of transmission. With the strong emergence of SIP based VoIP traffic then opens the door for new entrants to exploit the market with very small amount of investment.

VOIP- Retail trade

Retail trade is a safer and easier option then Wholesale Buying and Selling. With retail trade the procedure is based on successfully marketing the product to the general masses. In order to do this the following steps need to be taken care of:-

1) The retail market is literally the whole world the only issue is to integrate the different online payment mechanisms. So it is perhaps more important to know of the different payment mechanisms such as PayPal, Google Wallet, Online Banking. These payments are seamless in their integration with the VoIP software Billing Systems. However payments mechanisms such as Bitcoin should be avoided as this particular platform is totally unknown, unverified and hence cannot be trusted at all.
2) The practical way to approach is firstly to know which payment mechanisms you want to integrate with. Once the payment integration is done then you need to launch the Mobile Apps to make the calls. All this is dependent on successful Marketing.
3) In retail trade the most important aspect is quality, the voice quality has to be crystal clear and should connect the first time to any number in the world. So therefore it is essential that interconnections are made with multiple carriers such as WorldCom, TATA and Net2Phone. This will ensure that the call connects as long as the number is working. If one carrier route is not performing then call will automatically go onto the next carrier in the routing table.
4) The pricing should be competitive and this means that for any destination does not have a mark-up more than 15% since the money is made on traffic volume.
5) When making the rate sheet with all the destination codes and respective rates per min it is important to add the prefixes of

Premium Numbers. For example do not leave the UK as one prefix 44xxx rather add all the prefixes such as 441,4478,4470,44871,4490 and so on this will prevent those people who are actively searching for loopholes to call Premium Numbers in order to get a payout. Know that there is an active VoIP community members who are constantly opening accounts with VoIP carriers just to exploit the rate sheet. Whenever they find a destination sub prefix such as 44872 not added in the rate sheet they have the opportunity to exploit this. This gives the criminal minded the chance to call 44872 at the much lower rate of 4420 hence getting a healthy payout. One UK based International carrier added Bangladesh prefix as 88 rather than 880 and this was exploited by making calls to the satellite phone operator at a higher rate with the prefix 88 Thuraya. A simple mistake which was discovered after 1 month billing period left the company on the brink of bankruptcy.

6) There needs to be good customer service this also is a very important aspect of the business. It is ultimately the relationship with the client which will establish Brand loyalty. So therefore adequate resources need to be allocated to address the problems of the clients. And with the current digital age this means that the customer care is offered on multiple platforms such as Twitter, Email, Web Chat, Telephone and What's App.

7) The first impression of the company is normally the reflection of the company Website hence it is of vital importance that the website design is modern looking and up to date in terms of technical and fashion standards.

8) The last part is to advertise the website and start business.

This is the type of product that you will need to retail to your customers. The card can be digitally delivered.

VOIP- DID numbers

DID numbers are virtual numbers and this is what makes the global world a village. Any US or UK or Europe or any other country Virtual number can be mapped onto any IP Phone or Mobile APP. The benefits of this are that the local population of US can call that number at the local cheap rates to connect with the company. So this opens a very large market for the company and also gives the impression that the company is a Large Global Entity whereas in reality it may be just a small office with a single person.

Any business will look forward to utilize this feature and many companies are already offering this on a monthly subscription.

Also note the next time you see a local number displayed for any company do not assume that it is indeed a locally based company. Many people assume it is a local company and when they conduct financial transactions and thereafter are cheated they have absolutely no resort to justice. The company might have obtained the local DID number on false credentials normally requiring only a valid Email address.

With increased globalization, the demand for Virtual numbers will increase and the companies engaged in International trade can greatly benefit from these types of services.

VOIP – Mobile Based Apps

We are currently living in a time period where the Smart Phone is the first source of information, communication and the most useful tool in decision making. Mobile Applications are very important and serve an important connection with the clients.

In VOIP the Mobile APP is primarily used to make cheap calls over the Internet thus the client is able to save a significant amount. Calls through VoIP are a lot cheaper than using Mobile or Direct dial from PSTN lines, it can literally be a saving of 95%. For example to call the USA from Mobile from outside the USA it is easily more than 30 cents whereas calling through the VoIP dialer it is on average around 1-2 cents per minute.

This is a typical Mobile App which enables the user to call through VoIP and enjoy calls at reduced costs. The quality is dependent on the internet connection and if there is a good internet connection then the voice quality is better than direct calling through the Mobile Network.

VOIP – Software

The main software system which is required is the Billing Software System this has many features from among them:-

- Authentication of the accounts and the IP addresses.
- Announcing IVR minutes and balance
- Displaying connected calls and failed calls
- Billing the amount and the no of sec.
- Download of CDRs.
- Financial reports showing profits and loss.
- Billing tricks to deceive the clients. Client should not be naïve.

Some of the more expensive billing systems like Mera Switch, Digitalk and others which are used by high end Telco's have such a sophisticated system which can change routing when the quality parameters fall below the threshold.

So if the ASR (Average Success Rate) falls below 40% then the Billing system will automatically change the Route to a different carrier. Likewise if the ACD (Average Call Duration) on one carrier falls below the stipulated 4 Mins then the Billing system will automatically change the route to a different carrier.

So the more expensive billing options give a total piece of mind to the Carrier and the Telecoms Service Provider. This is a business which does not need daily a lot of effort except constant marketing.

Welcome admin@321 — About

Client
▷ Manage Client
▷ Manage Gateway
▷ Manage PIN
▷ Recharge Card

Rates and Destinations
▷ Voice Rate Plan
▷ Call Destination
▷ Voice Package

DID
▷ DID Calling Card
▷ DID For Outgoing Call
▷ Extension

Route Management
▷ Routing
  • Add
  • Search
  • Route Retry Config
▷ Call Simulator
▷ Manage Translation

Report
▷ Operational Report
▷ Finance & Accounts Report
▷ General Reports
▷ Log Report

Users And Other Settings
▷ Manage Users
▷ Manage Roles
▷ Manage Data System
▷ Manage Language
▷ Manage System Configuration
▷ Alarm Configuration
▷ MailServer Configuration
▷ Layout Configuration

Manage Partition
▷ Manage Switch Partition

Add Call Routes

Originating Client or Reseller	All	
My Switch (IP)		
Destination Code		
Destination Name		
Prefix	[Add] [Remove]	
Strip Prefix	0	if destination code is 008801 but you need to send terminator 8801, then you need to put Strip Prefix 2
Translated Dial Plan		if destination code is 008801 but you need to send to a terminator 1118801 then set Strip Prefix= 2 and terminating prefix 111
Route Gateway Type	● Carrier ○ Registerd User	
Terminating Client	access	
Terminating Prefix	[none]	Add Prefix
Terminating IP	108.161.137.121:506([Add]	
Added IPs	[Remove]	
Protocol	SIP	
Priority	1	1 gets priority over 2 and so on
Capacity	-1	-1 for unlimited concurrent call. For other capacity, please input the right number
Status	Enable	

[Reset] [Submit] [Advance]

Sidebar

- Voice Rate Plan
- Call Destination
- Voice Package

DID
- DID Calling Card
- DID For Outgoing Call
- Extension

Route Management
- Routing
  - Add
  - Search
  - Route Retry Config
- Call Simulator
- Manage Translation

Report
- Operational Report
- Finance & Accounts Report
- General Reports
- Log Report

Users And Other Settings
- Manage Users
- Manage Roles
- Manage Data System
- Manage Language
- Manage System Configuration
- Alarm Configuration
- MailServer Configuration
- Layout Configuration

Manage Partition
- Manage Switch Partition

Security
- Manage Ips

IM Management
- Manage IMBroadcast

Form

Destination Name		
Prefix		Add / Remove
Strip Prefix	0	if destination code is 008801 but you need to send terminator 8801, then you need to put Strip Prefix 2
Translated Dial Plan		if destination code is 008801 but you need to send to a terminator 1118801 then set Strip Prefix= 2 and terminating prefix 111
Route Gateway Type	● Carrier ○ Registerd User	
Terminating Client	access	
Terminating Prefix	[none] — Add Prefix	
Terminating IP	108.161.137.121:5060 Add	
Added IPs		Remove
Protocol	SIP	
Priority	1	1 gets priority over 2 and so on
Capacity	-1	-1 for unlimited concurrent call. For other capacity, please input the right number
Status	Enable	
Enabled LCR	☑	
Enabled Loss Less Routing	☐	
Stop Retry	☑	
Random Caller ID	☑	
Incoming CLI Prefix		If you want to change caller ID start with 880 or 00880 set 880||00880
Outgoing CLI Length	6 To 15	
Outgoing CLI Prefix		
Select Time Based	☑	

Day	Time(From)	Time(To)		
All	0	0	0	0	Add Remove

slot list:

QoS Alert: ☑

ACD	Below 4	Min	Above 10	Min	in last 2	Hour
ASR	Below 15.0	%	Above 50.0	%	in last 2	Hour
PDD	Below 1	sec	Above 8	sec	in last 2	Hour

Reset Submit Basic

Monitoring Report

From	23-9-2017 00:00:00
To	23-9-2017 23:59:59
Originating Client	All
Originating IP	All
Originating Country	All
Terminating Client	All
Terminating IP	All
Destination Code	All
Terminating Destination Code	All

General
- ○ Detailed — All
- ● Summary — None
- ○ Specific Report

Origination
- ☑ Customer
- ☑ IP
- ☑ Region
- ☑ Prefix
- ☐ Country

Termination
- ☑ Customer
- ☑ IP
- ☑ Region
- ☑ Prefix

Records Per Page: 30

[Reset] [Get Report] [Download]

Add Rate Plan

Rate Plan Name
Description
TAX (Percentage)   0.0

Options
○ From Rate Plan   [None]   Increase By(%) 0.0
○ From File   Browse... No file selected.
● Add Destination Wise

Reset   Submit

About

Add Calling Card DID

DID Number

Description
DID Type   ● Calling Card ○ Registration DID ○ Call Back DID
Allowed IP List

Add DID Outgoing Call

DID Number   [   ]   [Add] [Remove] [Browse]
                              [   ]

Description
DID Type   ⦿ Forward ○ Hot Dialing

Buying Cost Of DID   *Per DID*
⦿ None
○ Per Month   [0.0]
○ Per Call   [0.0]
○ Per Min   [0.0]

Selling Cost Of DID   *Per DID and Per Client*
⦿ None
○ Per Month   [0.0]
○ Per Call   [0.0]
○ Per Min   [0.0]

Expire Time   October ▾   2020 ▾

Select Client
Client   [   ]

                              [Reset] [Submit]

Profit Summary   *Today Till Now Report for All*

Report Span   ● Today Till Now   ○ Previous Day   ○ Previous 2 Days   ○ Custom Date Range
Report Type
    ○ Client Wise   All
    ○ Destination Wise   All
    ○ Hourly
    ○ Agent Wise   All
    ● DID Wise   All

[Get Report] [Download]

Copyright© Reve Systems. All rights res

Add Client

Client ID	
Password	Password length should be minimum 4 with a digit and letter
Confirm Password	
Client Type	◉ Reseller ◯ Originating ◯ Terminating ◯ Both
Reseller Type	◉ Rate based ◯ Comission based
Balance	0.00
Parent Account	[None]
Voice Rate Plan	[None] View Rate Increase By 0.0 %
Reseller Partition	[None]

Future Rate

Org Rate Plan Activation	Org Rate Plan Activation Date
	[None] View Rate 23-9-2017 1:9:37 [Add Next]

Account Information

Payment Type	◉ Prepaid ◯ Postpaid	
Credit Limit	0.00	
Maximum Allowed Calls	-1	-1 for unlimited calls
Max Client Limit	-1	-1 for unlimited client limit
Max Allowed Balance	-1.0	-1 to allow unlimited Balance to his clients
Role	[Default]	
Status	◉ Active ◯ Blocked	
Rate Plan Creation	◉ Enable ◯ Disable	
Enable Child IVR	◉ Enable ◯ Disable	
Client Permission	☑ Reseller and Pin ☐ IP Client	
IVR Language	English	
IVR Currency	USD	
Balance Alert	◯ Enable ◉ Disable	
Alert At Balance	0	
Auto Invoice	◯ Active ◉ Inactive	
Invoice Due Date	7	days

Contact Information

Name		
Designation		
Company Name		
Phone		
Mobile No		For password retrieval, this Mobile Number will be used
Email		For password retrieval, this email ID will be used
Fax		

Add Single PIN

PIN Number		Supports letter and digits
PIN Password		
Caller ID		
Pin Type	Rechargeable	
PIN Balance	0.0	
Payment Type	● Prepaid ○ Postpaid	
Parent Account	[none]	
Voice Rate Plan	[None]	View Rate Increase By 0.0 %
Pin Status	● Active ○ Block	
Activation Time	23-9-2017 00:00:00	
● Expire Time	23-9-2019 23:59:59	
○ Expire After First Use		Days
IVR Language	English	
IVR Currency	USD	
Call Record	○ Yes ● No	

DID Hot Dialing

Country	[Select]
DID	[Select] [Add] [Add All] [Remove]

[Reset] [Submit] [Basic]

The above is self-explanatory steps to create clients, create calling pins and shows the sophistication of one of the most stable yet cheapest VoIP Billing platforms. This is the Itel Billing system which is hosted on a UNIX server.

VOIP Hardware

The main uses for Hardware are either to use it as IPBX where basically 2 gateways of the same protocol are linked up to connect a remote branch to the Head Quarters. So if a company has several offices in different countries it can all operate under one PBX the IPBX by assigning different extensions to the different IP Phones and IP Gateways thus complete remove the long distance cost of calls. And all intra-branch communication is totally free just like in a hotel where one room can call another room for free cost. This is the real benefit of employing VoIP technologies and the call quality is totally dependent on the strength of the Internet connection. But voice is not like Video it does not require a lot of Bandwidth hence this solution can be implemented worldwide.

The other important use of VoIP hardware is to route Mobile Calls to the different mobile network. Many companies in Europe pay a significant amount to the local Telecom Providers for domestic Mobile calls. This cost can be reduced by using a GSM gateway which will route calls through to the different Mobile Networks from within their own network. So calls will be within the same network which is low cost or sometimes free for a monthly subscription rather than high costs calls through local PSTN carriers. So calls from within the same network 'Vodafone to Vodafone' are a lot cheaper than calls originating from BT Telecom to Vodafone. In this case there are no intra settlement termination costs and these benefits can be utilized by any company which has significant Telecoms costs.

The best hardware for immediate rate of return is the VoIP Termination Gateways alongside the Simbank. The cheapest Gateways are Chinese Made namely Sky Gateways and Dinstar. These are available as low as $350 for 16 ports GSM Gateway and with a total investment of about $500 a daily income of $500 can be made from reselling this route. Other more expensive options are available from Companies such as 2N which is based in Czech. These gateways are a lot more expensive and also more difficult to operate. Whereas the Chinese Gateways does not require any technical skill it's all plug and play mode.

This is a Chinese made GSM VoIP gateway which is approx. $700 and can terminate 8 simultaneous calls through the GSM network.

VOIP- the Premium Number market

The Premium number markets is worth billions of Dollars all Betting, Gaming, Dating, Consultancy is done through the Premium Numbers. And also the criminals operating in this field are on the constant hunt to make money through illegal means.

The illegal means are as follows:-

1) **Missed Calls** – Modern day gangsters are sending thousands of calls to foreign numbers per sec and these types of calls are Missed Call which means the call after the first ring is hung up. So the person whose number is dialed is forced to call back. Before he connects or the bell even rings the Premium Virtual Number is answered with a silent fake ring and the billing period starts. Before the caller even realizes what has happened to him 20 sec or more of credit has been stolen from him. This is billed at a very high rate which means all the subsequent people in the chain all benefit from this. So the proceeds of this are split by the Telecom companies and the original person who sent the Missed Calls. People normally target the poor segment of the society who makes assume a relative in need is calling them from a foreign country.

2) **Exploiting the rate sheet** – rate sheets are studied of all the Telecom companies and then this information in unethically exploited for financial gain. So for example if a new break out for a particular Premium rate destination is offered perhaps it is likely many carriers have not immediately updated their rate sheets to reflect these changes. So there is a discrepancy

between the rates charged for the call to the Premium number and the payout for the Premium number. So this discrepancy is exploited and all the traffic sent to that Premium number is profit until the rate sheet is updated or the Premium number prefix code is blocked.
3) **Mass SMS messages**. These fake messages normally congratulate the recipient of some lottery win or prize win. However the reality of this scam is that the Message only intends to engage with the recipient requesting him or her to ring back. When they ring back on a number which may resemble a normal standard they are asked to wait on the line which the background IVR is keeping them company. The longer they wait the more the fraudsters are making money, literally by the second.
4) Sometimes these scammers make adverts with unbelievable offers which are too good to be true however the reader is tricked into calling the Premium number.

An individual named Noor, who is a mastermind in Premium Number related fraud, is currently no 1 on the FBIs Technical Crime Wanted List. This person has international connections in many countries has successfully avoided prison through bribery. He channeled millions of dollars of fraudulent Premium number related payments.

The Premium Rate Industry works on unethical principles and it is well known that the Criminal is protected by the privacy laws which the legally registered company failed to disclose at time of legal enquiries.

VOIP – Fraud and ways to detect it

VoIP fraud is a big menace in the Industry many companies are forced to file bankruptcy when they have been victimized by organized criminal gangs. So many European and US based companies have been forced to close their operations after the criminal gangs have cheated them of millions of dollars.

Not all companies, some of the Governments are also cheated millions of dollars through the operation of illegal gateways. These illegal gateways bypass the legal channels thus denying the government of revenue.

So therefore this VoIP field matters to everyone the individual, the companies and the governments.

The different types of fraud which are unique in its nature are as follows:-

Wire Fraud- A Company with false credentials opens a Prepaid Termination accounts with a carrier and starts sending them traffic and makes prompt payment. After sometime there is some level of trust between the carrier and its client. At this point in time the client sends a large Telex Transfer Bank payment to the Bank account of the carrier. And the carrier credits the account of its client and the traffic is terminated by the carrier. However the payment does never reach since it's cancelled or it was on fake TT and thereafter the carrier is not able to do anything. So therefore it is very important for all carriers to scrutinize the documentation of any new Applicant.

DID changes- A client registers his telephone number access for cheaper calls through a carrier and he gives him primary number as the authorized number. The Carrier assumes this is just 1 channel number which means only 1 simultaneous calls can be placed. However the client from the network operator orders literally 100s of channels to be added onto that single authorized number and hence even a few hours of termination will result in heavy loss esp. if it is to high cost destinations or premium numbers.

Similarly a client has literally 100s of DIDs numbers mapped onto its main channels. When one of the authorized number is blocked due to non-payment of bills, the client automatically removes that particular DID number from the account so it is no longer the main CLI number. The new number will be the next in order of the DID range. So for example let's say the main DID number is 02076209100-9900 which is a range of 800 numbers, a full block of DID numbers. Once the main 02076209100 is blocked and blacklisted, the client will remove that number and replace it with 02076209110, which is again registered with the same carrier and the same cycle is repeated.

All these changes are literally made within minutes so therefore to detect this type of crime is very difficult and in this instance it is better to blacklist a whole DID range.

Termination fraud

This type of fraud is basically bypassing the legal transition route of any voice traffic to a particular country. There are basically 3 types of route available on the market:-

1) TDM route which is the fiber high quality route which most network operators use.
2) VoIP CLI route- this is the licensed route sold officially by the Network owner and its partners. So for example in the UK the network is owned by BT so its route is licensed and regulated by OFTEL, the official body governing the Telecoms Industry.
3) The third type is the NON-CLI Grey route which is the illegal cheap quality route to any country. This route is normally terminated through the GSM gateways and is on low quality codecs such as g723.1 and g729. This costs the national carriers a substantial amount in lost revenue.

The termination through illegal channels is a growing concern to the Network owned operators. And there are many software solutions employed by the network operators to detect this type of traffic, by looking at the traffic profile on the individual Sims, the rate of constant calls, the different types of random numbers dialed, the Sim being locked to a particular GSM tower, stationary Sim and non-movement, non-incoming traffic, non-use of SMS or internet services. All these indicators point to the fact that the Sim has been compromised and is used illegally for VoIP termination onto the local network.

How this works is that the international calls comes onto the VOIP GSM Gateway, the VoIP send the call to the GSM channel which is basically a mobile phone so the local Sim dials the local number. So therefore the cost of the call is a local call and not an international call. With the major difference between the call of the local calls and the international call – this is all pocketed by the illegal traffic setup.

This is a high risk operation and many people are arrested for this type of illegal traffic.

The Government authorities in order to tackle the Illegal VoIP termination need to monitor the traffic profile originating from the national GSM Sims. Also there needs to be strict biometric authentication for the issuing of Sims to the customers. Another form of detection is to send random calls through the many different carriers especially those who advertise the illegal non-Cli routes on the public forums.

PBX Hacking

One of the most important concerns for any business is to have completed Security that includes General IT security where most companies have adopted security measures to fight the threats of malicious viruses, Trojans and blackmail attempts. However what is neglected is that the commonly used IPBX/PBX which is the

Private Branch Telephone Exchange has very little security and is normally operating under default password and settings.

This gives the criminal the opportunity to exploit this weakness in the security settings of the PBX system and the consequences can be devastating. There is an active group of PBX hackers who the main media has chosen to ignore and this is not really emphasized by the specialists in the IT security industry.

What happens is that these individuals who have very little technical knowledge know some of the IVR numbers of the PBX. So it may be a customer service number or general telephone number. Outside office working hours, when these customer service numbers are dialed the caller is greeted and the IVR plays its normal message. During this call the Caller tries to retrieve the outside line which is normally worldwide done by pressing '9'. In order to overcome this Caller dials default password which normally consists of 4 digit pin and then presses 9 this gives it access to the outside International line.

Once the security is breached, the system is totally hacked and is at the mercy of its Hackers. The hackers will know how many lines are available at the PBX, so they get a dialer hosted on a private server to dial the IVR number of the PBX (customer service number) this is normally free phone number or cheap domestic cost. Thereafter the dialer dials the pin number and has complete access to the outside line. Now armed with 10's of channels the Dialer dials from within the PBX International Premium Numbers. These Premium Numbers are up to $1 per min. So over the weekend these Hackers literally pass through thousands of minutes and earn $30-40k for merely 2 days of illegal traffic. There is no way the Telecom Provider can trace the numbers or refuse to pay the Bill. The telecom companies all benefit from this traffic so therefore the company has to pay the bill or if it is insured the

Insurance Company will pay for it. But there is a collusion with the Criminals since this particular industry for a large extent caters for the Criminal minded people and all the people in the chain benefit.

So therefore it is important to have the PBX totally secure and ideally all international numbers should be blocked through direct dial. And also domestic traffic should be allowed so in the event it is hacked there is no financial incentive for the Hacker to pursue his criminal intent.

There is a famous gang operating from Milan, Italy who has earned millions of dollars through this PBX fraud targeting Mid-Sized communications. Sometimes a rogue employee of a particular company provides the inside details to the PBX network which allows it to be hacked over the weekend. This particular gang uses International Premium numbers to extract the funds out of the hacked PBX and this makes it very difficult for authorities to trace this type of crime.

VOIP- Security

VoIP security means that the full network connected to the VoIP should be secure this includes the software and the hardware. Since any intrusion will make any VoIP cripple within minutes.

As for the Software the biggest threat is the one from Hackers there are many gangs whom only desire to open a VoIP account with any company with the sole purpose of hacking into it. The VOIP Software which is based on Windows Platform can easily be hacked and the consequences are that the hacker will deplete all the funds of the carrier. Once an account or server is hacked it means the hacker is able to add new IPs, add balance to accounts and thereby terminate the traffic and pocket the money. Voipswitch from Poland has a very bad reputation as being hackable; despite its popularity it is one of the most hacked software's. Many people also use software's which are themselves hacked versions and not official licensed version, these type of software's are also hackable. So some carriers use the VOS3000 Software but they buy it online from unlicensed sellers and this is dangerous.

On the Hardware side the PBX system needs to be secure to prevent hacking attempts and the best option to fight this is to disable International calling from within the network. And any International calls should have a separate method of dialing or alternatively the network should be disabled at end of working hours. Also Switches and VOIP gateways can be hacked since most of them have some kind of web interface this is normally not secure as it is open on a Public IP. Once it is accessible on a Public IP it is hackable, and the hacker only needs to add a new IP which is authorized to terminate traffic. Before this is realized the damage is done.

VOIP- Financial fraud and how to prevent it.

Financial fraud is rampant in the Telecoms industry, this involves carriers sometimes being locked in a dispute over many issues including the CDR files, Billing accuracy, non-payment and wire fraud.

Some carriers are regularly targeted by Credit card fraudsters whom use stolen Credit Card details to load credit onto VoIP accounts and thereafter making calls to Premium numbers and pocketing the money.

Medium size carriers are targeted by company who are registered with the sole purpose of defrauding carriers by sending traffic based on fabricated TT details.

Larger carriers are also targeted by inducing them to open the network for mutual two way traffic but the route offered by the fraudster will not work and he will at the same time send traffic. He will restrict his own route by mixing with NON CLI routes, or restricting the no of channels.

Another reason for common disputes is that most carriers will resort to what is termed as mixing which basically selling a pure White Licensed route is mixed with an illegal Grey Non-Cli Route. This route is a lot cheaper quality and lower in terms of pricing. Many of the large carriers are also engaged in this unethical business practice, this practice is so widespread that finding a pure CLI route has become increasingly difficult.

Many of the VoIP calls have embedded encryption which means they can't be listened to by a third party so there is an element of privacy as opposed to calls originating from the PSTN or the Mobile network.

Online Marketing

Marketing is an integral part of any success story sometimes the product is mediocre but with intense aggressive marketing strategies it is built into a market leader. This is also very true in the Telecoms Industry in particular the VoIP; there is a lot of misinformation and hidden charges that the Telecoms Operators do not disclose.

Firstly we start with the billing software this has so many capabilities that can trick any intelligent customers. There are so many hidden charges on accounts such as daily maintenance fee, which is normally so insignificant that the customer will not even realize while his balance is depleted. Then there is the expiry period again another ploy to eat the balances in the customers' accounts. In addition to that there is the connection call charge so every successful call has a surcharge which the customer is oblivious to. Then there is the mid call charge which is normally at

5 Mins or 8 min intervals, a fixed amount is reduced from the accounts. Also there is the short minutes where every minute is actually only 50 sec so all these charges are actually deception to the customer, this is commonly implemented on all Calling Cards or those who advertise aggressive minutes.

To summarize the billing software deception we have the following:-

- Connection charges
- Mid Call charges
- Short Minutes
- Daily Maintenance Charges
- Expiry period
- Route Mixing with NON CLI routes.
- Premium number customer service rates.

To successfully market the product the companies tend to exaggerate the products which they are selling, the voice minutes.

In order to successful market all the Social Media platforms need to be utilized in order to make the brand successful. What this means is to use the following services and interact with potential clients:-

- Facebook page
- Twitter account
- Instagram
- Email/ Website /Blog
- Google adverts
- Forums general and specific
- What's App messaging
- SMS Messaging

No doubt to attract attention to any product is built on highlighting the main qualities and features of its product. The best way to build loyalty is by giving consistent high quality routes at any affordable rate.

Online Branding

Brand value is very important to get customer loyalty and this is done through allocating regular funds for advertising. This means to directly interact with all existing customers and giving those financial incentives to introduce new customers. This will build traffic and the client base very quickly since the one who is referring will see a financial incentive in terms of free credit. This is the most practical way of increasing business and there is no need to operate at a loss. Since the margin offered to the Referrer is the profit from the sale of credit to the new customer.

Reputable companies

In this business like any other it is important to do business with those companies who have a good reputation. Working with a strong partner will make your business stronger and it will no doubt strengthen your business model. Since if you interconnected with the world's leading carriers it will give the impression to the client that this is a reliable carrier, one that can be trusted.

The following is a list of reputable carriers who offer many types of Telecom solutions :-

- IBasis
- TATA
- World Com
- BelgaCom
- Sprint
- Vonage
- AT&T
- Verizon
- Telenor
- Level 3 Communications

Trade Fairs

In order to know the best in the field and the leading innovative companies then it is important to have some kind of real life experience with the largest Telecom Companies. Every country will have its own Trade Fair where the latest technology is displayed; the major decision makers of the major companies are present. With this there is an opportunity to build a personalized relationship with existing companies and other companies. Also it opens the horizons and allows the person to engage in Business to Business agreements.

Some of the useful Trade Fairs where many Medium Size Telecom companies participate are as follows:-

- Gitex, based in Dubai this is the new hub for Business. http://www.gitex.com/en/sectors/gulfcomms/

"The BYOD and enterprise mobility market size is estimated to grow from $35.10 billion in 2016 to $73.30 billion by 2021. Business leaders and employees alike want more mobile-first solutions"

- SibTelecom & IT Novosibirsk
  http://www.seexpo.com/index.php/index/Search/industry/fid/72/sid/250

Practical Step-by-Step for VOIP termination

The following is the simple method of starting VoIP termination in any country where it is legal to operate through Sim card or through the PSTN networks:-

1. Premises with decent Internet connection with public IPs from the ISP. It can be a house or a flat since only limited space is required.
2. Full knowledge of all the local tariffs and packages. So for GSM Sims then one should know what package is the cheapest, which one gives free daily minutes, free monthly minutes. Similarly the PSTN network which calls is free.

3. Which gateway is required and to order the gateway according to the capacity. Is digital Gateway required which can connect directly to ISDN 30e or E1 (30 channels) or T1 (24 Channels) or GSM Gateway with capacity of 8, 16, 30 channels.
4. Purchasing the Sims/ PSTN topped up with the necessary credit.
5. Configuration of the GSM / Digital Gateway to accept VoIP traffic from a Public Switch IP. Configuration on the Switch (such as Itel Switch) and entering the buyers IP and the Sellers IP (GSM Gateway IP).
6. Making all the settings on the software billing system such as allowed no of simultaneous calls (capacity), pricing per minutes and the routing table.
7. Agreement with the buying carrier with the payment schedule and banking details.

Practical Step-by-Step for VOIP Origination Calling Cards, Sim Cards

VoIP origination means collecting retail traffic or wholesale traffic and then terminating this to a Telecoms carrier. Most of the Retail traffic is from Mobile phone direct dialing this is at least 150% more expensive than the actual cost of the call. In order to collect this traffic a Mobile dialer needs to be used which will send the call through the Internet rather than the Mobile network thus bypassing the Mobile Network charges and terminating on a more competitive independent network. In order to setup a fully-fledged Telecoms company which offers the best calling rates combined with the best quality the following steps need to be followed:-

1. Firstly you need a UNIX server with billing software installed along with Public IP.
2. Then you need to register the IP and interconnect with some A_Z Tier 1 Carriers which has multiple routes at different pricing.
3. Now you need to make a strategy of how to market the Calling card what billing parameters to use such as per sec billing, per minute billing, etc. And set the rate sheet for the voice based products.
4. Design the brand along with the website and the dialer on the Apple Store and the Google Play Store.
5. Market the dialer on all the social media platforms with aggressive marketing techniques offering free minutes to those who refer customers whom purchase credit worth $10 or so.
6. The billing software with the rate sheets for the wholesale carriers uploaded and the retail rates uploaded will show all the statistics for every day. The Control Panel will show daily minutes terminated, daily dollar usage, daily profits and costs. And this can be generated for per week or per month or for any period of time.

Cost Analysis

The cost analysis can be broken down as follows for the simplest operations for Origination and Termination.

Origination Costs

- Unix Server $250 per month
- Software billing system $3000 plus $450 yearly support charges after the 1st Year.
- Dialer purchase and unique branding $2000.
- Prepaid Credit with the Tier 1 Carriers $1000.
- Requires 1 full time worker who will overlook every aspect of the business.

Termination Costs

- Unix server $350 per month with Hosted Billing Software
- GSM Gateway starting from $500
- Sims or PSTN starting from $500.
- Internet Bandwidth with VPN capabilities $100.
- Requires 1 Fulltime worker to monitor the traffic and update the credits etc.

Rate of Return: Economic Analysis

The economic analysis is that the greatest rate of return is for the Premium Rates numbers which is legalized fraud against the end user, thereafter the Termination of Traffic which again is illegal in some countries and then the Origination of Traffic.

Whatever the case whichever carries has collected traffic of any kind will no doubt earn a good amount as he literally earns every second. And the cost of operations is very low it does not require legal license, shop or retail points, many workers, high level of expertise. So therefore overall it is more beneficial than many other online trades and definitely the most rewarding for the one who has secured some good clients and connections.

Traffic will grow very fast if Resellers are appointed and they will have their own unique Brand and this will greatly help the cause of the main carrier. All Billing software's have the ability to create N Level of Resellers so this means the potential of doing business is vast and there are no restrictions whatsoever. Whoever has an Internet connection, a Smart Phone is a potential customer, anywhere in the World. Perhaps the only single restriction is the current financial regulations and the state of banking operations where intra-country banking is still not sophisticated and subject to hefty security regulations.

Anyone who is able to couple the financial demands of the client with the communication needs of the client is definitely a winner and no one can compete with him in the current market. So with the fast development of easy money transfer schemes through SMS banking, Online International banking there is potential the whole world market will be opened up very soon.

As long as the money is rotating then you have nothing to worry about, the fixed costs of operating this business for very low.

Common Mistakes

Common mistakes are those made by many carriers which hinders their growth and subjects them to a high risk strategy. On the internet trust is a very rare commodity and credentials can't be adequately verified hence precaution is necessary.

Secondly the internet market place is usually very competitive so therefore do not waste your time trying to sell a product which is overly priced.

Thirdly a good marketing strategy is the key to success rather than adopting a hi-tech product with all the features.

Finally be patient you will never know when the opportunity to make mega fast money will come. Since the market is moving very fast all the time, demand and supply are changing all the time so if you persist then that opportunity will come.

Investment Required – equipment, software and purchasing power.

In order to start this trade whether its origination or termination an investment of $4000 is normally sufficient and it's possible to recover this amount within the first month.

The greatest investment is the effort and the time required to make links.

Geographical based trends

The general geographical trends are as follows:-

Termination business is normally concentrated in them countries where the International call rate into the country is usually very high this means there is a greater incentive to terminate calls through the GSM gateway. The main countries are most African countries, Cuba and most South American countries. In some of these countries VoIP is banned but in others it is allowed to a certain degree if there is no alternative backbone or the Government does not have specific legislation with regards to this. For example the rate to Cuba is high as 50 cents per min and many Cubans reside in the US so therefore there is a lot of domestic US traffic to Cuba.

As for Origination traffic then the greatest demand is normally in them countries where there is a lot of migrant workers or tourists. Migrant workers will regularly call back home to their countries and likewise tourist will call back home even at higher than usual rates. So therefore partnering with these 2 segments of the society will yield beneficial results for many companies. And making agreements with Tourism based companies and operators and providing them with an own branded Dialer will normally yield good quick results.

Other Telecom services like DID are more likely to be utilized by large and medium size companies.

Real Life Examples of Success

Here I will highlight the success stories of two individuals whom learnt this trade from scratch and the purpose of this that it will serve as a motivation for the reader. The key thing is determination to succeed and when a person is equipped with knowledge and beneficial tips the person is increasingly confident.

1. This is a brief story of an individual named Shakeel who came from a remote village from the Province of Punjab, Pakistan. He got an intermediate certificate from the local high school and was able to communicate in broken English. He like many

of his country fellows wanted a gateway to easy life so headed for Europe. He came to settle in Germany. He could not find a job as he was not fluent in the local language so he thought of trying his chances on the Internet. He came across people doing Telecoms so decided to become a reseller for one of the local companies. This meant selling calling cards for a commission.

He sold many Calling cards to the migrant workers and started to network to other areas and other countries. He would take very little commission so he basically undercut other official resellers of the same company. So if the company offered him a commission of 10% he was willing to work for even 5% which meant that he was the preferred provider of these highly sought Calling cards. With dedicated customer service and consistency after one year he had generated enough sales. Now all the other companies wanted to know him too so they offered him their cards with higher attractive rates and commission. So he began to sell them cards to his clients. After becoming the main provider in his locality he decided to visit the companies to learn about the technical aspect of the business. After knowing the simplicity of this business he decided to get his own server and buy his own direct routes from the carriers and he already had a large client base. He transferred all his clients onto the new server, to his newly found company. Then he started an aggressive marketing campaign by offering free Mins to every referral like this he accumulated many more clients. He started operating in all the main cities and in all the adjacent countries. And within 5 years he was earning more than $90,000 per month. I had provided him with his first VoIP billing system with the Server and TATA routes.

2. The second individual came to me while I was in Kuwait, he was a young accountant aged around 27 and he wanted a reseller account on a VoIP Switch Server. I made the reseller account within 5 Mins and gave him the account details and gave him the reseller rates of the 5 countries which most of the migrant workers are from. He started selling at the same rates to all the shops and appointed individuals as resellers under him. In a few weeks' time he came again for another reseller account on a different billing system. He did the same procedure till he had 9 different billing system and 9 different reseller accounts with me. The impression he gave in the market was every product was different and from a different source. He gave the impression the market is highly competitive and this was a deterrent to any new comer. Also the different billing system has different features which he managed to exploit to his benefit. Within 2 years he had generated more than 1 million Mins per day from all the 9 servers. And after 3 years in the trade he was making $10000 per day in profit. He went on to establish schools in his home country and opened a chain of restaurants. To this day his main source of income is Telecoms.

Business Case Study

The intent is to interconnect with the big carriers and buy and sell voice minutes and other services. There is a strong business case for providing wholesale minutes to the European carriers and at the head of them Belgacom and BT. The Telecommunications sector is the fasted growing sector in the World and the need for communication is a fundamental need for every individual in this digital world.

Belgacom is currently buying low grade blended routes from International carriers based in London such as TATA. These carriers do not offer high grade premium pure TDM CLI routes rather they blend them with cheaper low grade grey illegal routes. I myself have called to destinations like Pakistan, India, Morocco, Afghanistan, and Nigeria through the Belgacom network and found the call is terminated with a grey illegal simcard. However these carriers sell at the same rate as Premium routes providing low or bad quality routes which adversely affect the revenue of Mobile Phone Operator. When the voice quality is low then demand for it is also low then it has negative consequences for Mobile Operator customers and its future business.

It is important for any Network Operator such as BT, Vodafone and Belgacom to maintain high quality routes and not to use mixed blended routes which is a form of cheating by the Wholesale carriers. We should make sure we offer the best routes by directly connecting with the Network Operators in the different countries and not allowing any mixing of the route and ensuring every call is of high voice, good ASR and high ACD thus increasing profits for STC.

There is a very high demand for call coming into Pakistan '92 prefix Traffic' and this is sold on the international market by these Carriers at a higher price with high profit margin of up to 25%. The International traffic to Pakistan is millions of minutes per day.

Similarly the outgoing traffic from Greek/Turkish customers to A_Z destinations abroad is also very high due to the fact there are a lot of expatriates and visitors from many different countries. Belgacom is buying minutes for these destinations for these Wholesale carriers at inflated rates and poor quality as the carriers aim to maximize revenue by way of blending white with illegal grey routes.

One has the opportunity to come into the market and offer better services meaning pure CLI TDM routes, at better pricing which is mutually beneficially to us and the carrier.

This is an industry which is worth millions of dollars revenue per day and profit literally starts from the very first minute. I will show projections of profitability based on 3 levels of traffic.

Profit Projections

Demand for Tunisia route is dependent on the rate per minute of the Tunisia route. However assuming the Tunisia wholesale rate termination rate is 0.07 USD per minute then based on traffic of 1 million minutes per day. We have daily usage of $70,000.

If we assume the profit margin is 0.01 USD per minute then we have monthly profit of $300,000.

Similarly if we sell routes to Tunisia and for each route add 0.01 per minute and based on 1 million minutes we have a monthly profit of $300,000. Total profit for each month -buying and selling is $600,000.

We can also expand and provide similar services to the other network operators based in any country.

The following table shows the monthly profit based on different levels of traffic (both buying and selling) and different profit margins. It clearly shows there is a lot of potential in this business. And in some case the Profit margins can be as much as $0.10 cents per minute.

| Mins per month/ | $0.01 | $0.0150 | $0.02 | $0.025 |

Profit margin on min	profit on Each minute	profit	profit	
15000,000(500k/day)	$150,000	$225,000	$300,000	$375,000
30,000,000(1000k/day)	$300,000	$450,000	$600,000	$750,000
45,000,000(1.5mil/day)	$450,000	$675,000	$900,000	$1,125,000
60 million/month(2 million per day)	$600,000	$900,000	$1,200,000	$1,500,000

Technical issues

It is a requirement that all routes are monitored 24/7 to ensure constant quality and the ASR rate is maintained and also ACD rates are high. These two are the parameters by which quality is established.

There will be constant maintenance of the Switch and the Billing system and backup servers to collect data. We are able to perform these actions and do the necessary maintenance.

Conclusion

I have come to the conclusion that the VoIP industry will completely replace the traditional PSTN based form of voice transmission since it is more efficient and cheaper to terminate. With worldwide access to the Internet infrastructure this means it is an exciting time to enter into this field. Combined with worldwide deregulation and privatization of the Telecom sector this is the time to enter into this lucrative business. There are many opportunities in the countries where the development is still on-going and there is a lot of global migration which means the demand is increasing all the time.

With the globalization of the systems including the Banking sector and the Telecommunications sector it means the world market is truly at your fingertips.

Some of the platforms are good for VoIP such as the IPhone play store and Google Play Store the only issue is that they take too much commission. If the service providers can negotiate favorable terms with some of these platforms then it will open up the market worldwide.

Countries which are dependent upon the revenue from the Settlement rates normally have high termination rates. These countries will always suffer from Illegal termination operations by organized gangs since the incentives are lucrative and rate of return is immediate and fast.

Countries which have oligopolistic Telecom industry will also have new competition from the Internet based carrier which cannot be defeated since it is not physically visible and the laws of the country may not apply to those who operate from outside the country. Thus origination should be welcomed and this will ultimately benefit the end user who can pay rates which are a lot less than the Telecom operator.

No doubt there is a real threat from the Apps which offer free calling like Telegram, What's App this will eventually replace the way voice communications are handled. Voice will become like text which means for a fixed monthly fee people will be able to communicate for unlimited minutes anywhere in the world. When that realization is reached the commodity for sale would not be the 'Voice Minutes' but 'Internet Bandwidth'. However for the developing world that realization is still a distant dream so African, South American and some Asian countries still offer good opportunities in this exciting VoIP arena.

For those who require specific consultancy on telecom related issues then please email me at: mmmtelecoms@gmail.com

23rd September 2017.

www.ingramcontent.com/pod-product-compliance
Lightning Source LLC
Chambersburg PA
CBHW020710180526
45163CB00008B/3021